W9-BZD-119

Paul Zindel

The Library of Author Biographies™

PAUL ZINDEL

Susanna Daniel

The Rosen Publishing Group, Inc., New York

For my mother

Published in 2004 by The Rosen Publishing Group, Inc.
29 East 21st Street, New York, NY 10010

First Edition

Library of Congress Cataloging-in-Publication Data

Daniel, Susanna.
Paul Zindel / Susanna Daniel.—1st ed.
   p. cm.— (The library of author biographies)
Summary: Discusses the life and work of author Paul Zindel, including his writing process and methods, inspirations, a critical discussion of his books, biographical timeline, and awards. Includes bibliographical references and index.
ISBN 0-8239-4524-3 (library binding)
1. Zindel, Paul—Juvenile literature. 2. Authors, American—20th century—Biography—Juvenile literature. 3. Staten Island (N.Y.)—Biography—Juvenile literature. 4. Children's stories—Authorship—Juvenile literature. [1. Zindel, Paul. 2. Authors, American.]
I. Title. II. Series.
PS3576.I518Z64 2003
812'.54—dc22

                                                            2003012422

Manufactured in the United States of America

Text from *About This Author: Paul Zindel*, from RandomHouse.com, reprinted with permission by Random House.

Text from *Humor, Bathos, and Fear: An Interview with Paul Zindel*, by Terri Lesesne, reprinted with permission by *Teacher Librarian*, Vol. 27, No. 2, December 1999, pp. 60–62.

Text from Scholastic.com, interview with Paul Zindel, reprinted with permission from Scholastic, Inc.

Table of Contents

Introduction:
The Birth of a
New Type of Book

In the 1970s, the young adult book publishing business grew dramatically when publishers realized that if they produced books for young people in paperback format instead of hardcover, the books would be less expensive to buy and distribute. Today, tens of millions of books for young adult readers are sold in the United States and Canada each year. Author Paul Zindel's thirty-odd novels comprise a small but significant portion of those sales.

Zindel wrote his first novel for young adults in 1968, when he was working as a high school science teacher in New York. The novel was called *The Pigman*, and it was about two teenagers who, lacking guidance from parents or teachers, befriend an old man, then end up betraying him. After, they must learn to take responsibility for their actions, and they learn a lesson from the experience. *The Pigman* was a success with readers and critics as soon as it hit bookstores, and it signaled the start of a career that would span more than thirty years, until the author's death in 2003.

From one novel to the next, Zindel develops unique teenage characters in difficult but realistic situations—such as homelessness, troubled families, broken homes, and alienation at school. The plots of his novels differ widely, but some of the themes are examined again and again.

In many of Zindel's young adult novels, adolescent characters search for a sense of identity or self-worth, which they are able to form only after enduring the mistreatment or neglect of other people. In *The Girl Who Wanted a Boy* (1981), for example, fifteen-year-old automechanics whiz Sibella Cametta has fallen in love for the first time. Unfortunately, the object of her affection is a bad-tempered and emotionally disturbed older boy named Dan, who does not return her feelings. Sibella's mother doesn't take her daughter seriously at all and her sister misguidedly pays a strange boy to pretend he likes Sibella so that she will forget about Dan. Sibella feels lonelier at home than anywhere else. Not until she makes a huge sacrifice for Dan and he breaks her heart can Sibella start to understand that she is not responsible for her family's flaws. She realizes that there is no rush; she has many years ahead of her, and she possesses qualities many people will love.

Other characters in many of Zindel's novels are misunderstood by adults and peers and long for a parental role model. This describes Chris Boyd, the misfit protagonist of *Confessions of a Teenage Baboon* (1977). Chris's father left him and his mother when Chris was a child, and his mother works as a nurse for terminally ill patients. In the novel, Chris must cope with the stifling attentions of a disturbed thirty-year-old man—the son of one of his mother's patients— who tries to become a father figure to him. He also must confront issues of death and abandonment when the man commits suicide.

The protagonist of Zindel's *The Amazing and Death-Defying Diary of Eugene Dingman* (1987) also lacks a father figure. Fifteen-year-old Eugene Dingman writes daily letters to the father who left him when he was nine years old, painstakingly and passionately chronicling his adventures working as a summer waiter at a resort in the Adirondack Mountains. Sadly, his father never responds, and Chris must learn to appreciate life without his father's support and love.

Though he is best known for his realistic, candid, and humorous depictions of troubled teenagers, late in his career Zindel switched to writing adventure books aimed at teens, which were different from anything he'd published before. Unlike his earlier novels, these books are fast-paced page-turners that rely more heavily on the plots of the stories than on the characters. Zindel's adventure novels have been compared to Peter Benchley's *Jaws* (1974), the classic shark thriller that inspired the film of the same name, and also to the work of R. L. Stine, the best-selling author of horror books for teenagers, including the *Goosebumps* and *Fear Street* series, which have been published steadily over the last fifteen years. Zindel's adventure novels attract a different audience than his earlier novels do; even adolescents who don't care much for reading enjoy Zindel's vivid descriptions of beastly predators and exciting battles for survival.

Zindel has won numerous awards for his work, including the distinguished Young Adult

Library Service Association's Margaret A. Edwards Award, which honors lifelong and enduring excellence in writing for young adults, and the Assembly on Literature for Adolescents Award for contributions to young adult literature, both of which he won in 2002, the year before his death.

Zindel is known as one of the most honest and courageous writers for teenagers. While adult critics have at times been less than thrilled with his negative portrayals of authority figures—many of his characters' parents and teachers are insensitive, mentally ill, or inattentive—his novels remain popular with teen readers.

One reason teenagers like Zindel's books is because the author doesn't talk down to his readers or pretend they are naive. Zindel doesn't seem to believe that adults are always dependable, or that teenagers are always careless, or that school is always worthwhile. In a world that can be so unreliable, teenagers are often left to figure out many of life's questions for themselves.

1 Life on Staten Island

There's a reason why Paul Zindel can write with sensitivity, compassion, and humor about teenagers coping with desperate circumstances—he was once a desperate teenager himself. "All of my novels begin with real, specific moments from my own life,"[1] Zindel said in an interview. Loneliness, coping with death and illness, feeling misunderstood, struggling to form a strong sense of self—these are some of the situations the author dealt with when he was an adolescent.

Paul Zindel was born on Staten Island, New York, in 1936. His father, Paul Sr., was a police officer, and his mother, Beatrice, was a homemaker. When Paul Jr. was two years old, his father left the family to move in with another woman. Paul Sr. all but disappeared, and Paul Jr. saw his father only ten more times before the man died in 1957. Beatrice was left penniless, lonely, and unskilled. She tried her hand at a number of careers, including nursing, real estate, running a hot dog stand, and inventing. She was constantly in search of a new way to get rich quickly. She also struggled with depression and bouts of paranoia.

Restless and searching for better work, Beatrice moved the family fifteen times before Paul was sixteen years old. As a result, he never formed any close friendships with kids his own age. When she was working as a nurse for terminally ill patients, Beatrice sometimes took in clients as boarders, but she tended to treat her patients without compassion and respect. She believed she was being cheated by the low wages and tedious nature of her job, and from time to time she even stole from patients. She justified her actions by claiming that she was not fairly compensated for her labor. Over the years, Beatrice's paranoia and depression kept her from inviting people to visit, so the apartment was usually a vacant and gloomy place. "Our house was a house of fear," Zindel would later say in an interview. "Mother never trusted anybody."[2]

His mother's mistrust of people made Paul feel like the world was out to get him, and because there was never anyone around to talk to, young Paul became an introvert and was shy and insecure with other people. He also became a sharp observer of the world around him. Left alone to explore whatever Staten Island neighborhood they happened to live in at the time, Paul entertained himself by producing puppet shows and creating cycloramas, or miniature stage sets, in cardboard boxes. He kept aquariums and terrariums, where small animals or plants live, and went to see movies whenever he could afford it. He lacked the athletic ability of some of his peers, but he developed an interest in the study of science. As he would later recall, "What a great love I had of microorganisms, of peering at worlds framed and separate from me."[3] As the years passed, Paul's social abilities remained weak, but his keen observation skills and sharp imagination flourished.

In an interview, Zindel explained that the place where he grew up had a remarkable influence on his childhood. "Staten Island was very unusual," he said. "It had many different towns, like Europe had. It had interesting woods to hide in, to chase animals in, and to fish in. There was an airport in my backyard, where we used to beg the pilots to take us up in all these sorts of incredible aircraft—open cockpit, two-winged airplanes that do loops and spins. And all of these things made their way into my books."[4]

Perhaps the most stunning fact about Paul Zindel's childhood is that he almost never read books. He didn't attend a professional play until he was in high school and didn't see a Broadway play until he had written several plays himself. Most writers are avid readers from early childhood and are heavily influenced by the books they loved. Zindel's training as a writer relied not on studying books but in observing life—people as well as microorganisms—and in exercising his imagination. "By the time I was ten," said Zindel, "I had gone nowhere, but had seen the world. I dared to speak and act out my true feelings only in fantasy and secret. That's probably what made me a writer."[5]

Paul started developing his playwriting skills earlier than his fiction-writing skills. In his first year or two of high school, he performed in a few school productions and wrote a handful of skits for student performances. As he later noted, "Some of my classmates got the impression I had a strange sense of humor—'macabre,' I believe, was the term they used. A group of student officers asked me to create a hilarious sketch for an assembly to help raise money. I decided that even if I could not succeed in the real world, perhaps my appointed role in life was to help other people succeed."[6]

Without realizing it at the time, Paul took another large step toward his eventual career during high school. With a friend named Richard Cahill, he wrote a short story called "A Geometric Nightmare," which was published in the school newspaper, *The Crow's Nest*. It would be more than a decade before Paul would return to writing fiction, but when he did, he would recall that first published story and marvel at how things work out. He never imagined that his writing would one day be wildly successful with the same audience that read *The Crow's Nest*: teenagers.

Adolescence Interrupted

Before he would get the chance to succeed as a writer, however, Paul had to overcome some difficult obstacles. In 1951, when he was a solitary fifteen-year-old with few friends and no girl-friend—and pining terribly for both—he contracted tuberculosis (TB), a respiratory disease. TB is much less common in the United States and Canada today than it was in the 1950s, when treatment drugs had only recently been discovered. The disease is caused by a bacteria that spreads through the air when someone sneezes or coughs, and the symptoms include terrible coughing fits, pain in the chest, fatigue, chills and fever, and weight loss. Paul was in no shape to attend school, and the TB was contagious, so he was put in a convalescent home, where ill people go to recover, and he lived there for eighteen months. His friendless and unstable home life had been challenging enough—but home had been pretty social compared to the convalescent center, where there were no other patients who were even close to Paul's age.

As you might expect, this period of recovery and isolation had a profound effect on the young author. Besides being lonely, life in the convalescent home was boring compared to his private adventures in his Staten Island neighborhood. In essays and interviews he would later write and give about his childhood, Zindel chose not to say much about his convalescence, except to recall that it was in the treatment center that he became fascinated with the work of the Polish composer Frédéric Chopin, in particular with a piece called the Warsaw Concerto. While recovering, he lived in his imagination, exercising it as vigorously as he had before he was sick, and when he finally returned to high school, he wrote an original play about an ill pianist who recovers in time to play the Warsaw Concerto at Carnegie Hall. The play earned a prize in a contest sponsored by the American Cancer Society, and Paul was awarded a fancy pen for his efforts.

Paul had attended four different high schools by the time he graduated in 1954. Soon after, he enrolled in Wagner College on Staten Island and majored in chemistry. To mix up his curriculum a little bit, he took a playwriting course from Edward Albee, who would go on to win three Pulitzer Prizes in drama, including one for *Who's Afraid of Virginia Woolf?* (1962), which was made into a classic film starring Elizabeth Taylor and Richard Burton. Zindel found Albee's teaching inspiring and was motivated to change his major from chemistry to literature and drama. The college wouldn't let him switch majors because he was on scholarship for chemistry, but he continued to be mentored by Albee and was always grateful for the time the teacher spent with him. During his senior year of college, Zindel wrote his second full-length play, *Dimensions of Peacocks* (1955), about a disturbed teenager whose overbearing mother works as a nurse and steals monogrammed linen napkins from her patients' homes. This play might have been the first time Zindel wrote directly from his personal experiences, but it would not be the last.

The Big Break

After graduating from college, Zindel used his science background to get a job as a technical writer for six months, but he hated the work and felt unfulfilled. He left technical writing to become a teacher of physics and chemistry at Tottenville High School on Staten Island. He remained at Tottenville from 1960 through 1969, a period during which he continued to write plays (two were staged in New York with little success, including *Dimensions of Peacocks*) and he became an avid theatergoer. He was inspired particularly by the plays of Tennessee Williams, whose passionate work revolves around self-destructive and desperate characters struggling to improve their lives. (Tennessee Williams wrote *A Streetcar Named Desire*, which in 1951 was made into a film starring screen legend Marlon Brando. Another Williams play that remains famous and widely read today is *The Glass Menagerie*, which was written in 1950.)

In 1964, Zindel's fourth and most successful play, *The Effect of Gamma Rays on Man-in-the-Moon Marigolds*, premiered at the Alley Theater in Houston. The play is about a bright adolescent girl named Tillie and her struggle to preserve her self-esteem in the midst of her mother's abuse and her epileptic sister's deviousness and competitiveness. For her school science project, Tillie raises marigolds that have been exposed to radiation. Some of the marigolds are stunted by the poison while some bloom beautifully, becoming a metaphor for her own poisonous family life. The marigolds give Tillie hope that she might thrive despite her stifling family. And it is clear at the end of the play that Tillie will blossom, while her sister will continue to be a victim of their mother's misery. *Marigolds* earned Zindel a number of prestigious honors, including the New York Drama Critics Circle Award for Best American Play of the Year (1970), the New York Critics

Award (1971), and the Pulitzer Prize in Drama (1971). The play was even made into a trimmed-down television version in 1966.

Marigolds opened off-Broadway—which is the next best thing to Broadway—in 1970 and moved to Broadway a year later. In the introduction to one edition of the play, Zindel wrote that after a decade of failure as a playwright, *Marigolds* practically wrote itself. Zindel later noted that the play is probably autobiographical since whenever he saw a production of it, he would laugh and cry more than everyone else there. He admitted that Tillie's unbalanced mother is based on his own—they even have the same name, Beatrice—but he added that unlike the fictional character, his own mother was capable of enormous love and compassion. Critics were crazy about *Marigolds*; they called it "splendid," "sublime," "touching," and "funny." They said it combined intelligence with passion, and humor with anguish in a way that charmed audiences of all ages.

Based on the success of *Marigolds*, it's easy to look back and see that Zindel might become a successful writer of novels for young people—after all, he obviously had an ear for adolescent characters and an understanding of their struggles.

At the time, however, Zindel needed some encouragement. He received just what he needed from a well-respected children's book author named Charlotte Zolotow. Zolotow appreciated Zindel's honest and compassionate portrayal of *Marigolds'* adolescent protagonist and saw the potential for a bright future in novel writing. Soon after, with Zindel's help, Zolotow would become crucial in developing the children's book division at Harper & Row, an important New York publishing house (now HarperCollins), and in influencing the fate of young adult literature forever.

A New Genre

As recently as thirty-five years ago, when Zindel was at the very dawn of his novel-writing career, realistic and honest books written for middle graders and teenagers did not exist. Books written for young people prior to the 1960s—called "junior novels" back then—portrayed stereotypical adolescents with idealistic lives and petty problems. Unlike many teens in real life, these well-adjusted teenage characters were surrounded by supportive parents, friends, and schoolteachers. Because they didn't reflect real life, junior novels were dismissed as fluff, or frivolous entertainment, and were not given the status or attention of important literature. Popular film and television programs were much the same during this time in history, and the overwhelming majority of TV families were depicted as successful, healthy, and happy.

Maybe you've seen old episodes of programs like *The Brady Bunch*, *The Partridge Family*, and *Happy Days*, all of which were produced in the late 1960s and early 1970s. In shows like these, as in the junior novels of the era, concerns like divorce, drugs, peer pressure, depression, and loneliness were practically nonexistent. Of course, these problems existed in the real world at the time, but they weren't usually revealed in popular media. Perhaps this was because the public was nostalgic for a simpler way of life and preferred not to acknowledge many social problems.

Charlotte Zolotow, the editor who encouraged Zindel to write novels for teens, was not interested in publishing more junior novels. She believed that Zindel had a talent for showing teenagers as they really are, which is often desperate, angry, sensitive, and longing for love. At her urging, Zindel started reading some popular teenage novels and found, in his words:

> There weren't many writers who were getting through . . . What I saw in most of [the books] had no connection to the teenagers I knew [from teaching]. I thought I knew what kids would want in a book, so I made a list and followed it.[7]

To brainstorm ideas for stories about teenagers, Zindel went directly to the source: his high school students. In an interview for *Teacher Librarian* magazine, he spoke casually about the humble beginnings of what turned out to be a stunningly successful career.

> I found out that in a group of a hundred boys, only two or three had read a single book. That book was always *Catcher in the Rye* [by J. D. Salinger, 1951]. Sometimes one of the boys had read a second book. That was always *Lord of the Flies* [by William Golding, 1954]. I asked the boys why they read those books and they told me it was because their girlfriends made them read it. I realized fairly quickly that there weren't many books around that showed age protagonists in a modern reality concerned with realistic problems.[8]

Zindel had no idea how important this realization would become in his own life and in the world of literature and publishing. Most critics give credit to two books that were printed in the late 1960s (both of which are still widely read) for fundamentally changing the way novels are written for preteens and teens. The first is S. E. Hinton's *The Outsiders* (1967), and the second is Paul Zindel's *The Pigman* (1968). *The Outsiders*, which is about a close-knit gang of social outcasts, was made into a movie in 1983 starring Tom Cruise, Matt Dillon, Rob Lowe, and Diane Lane, all of whom have gone on to become famous actors. *The Pigman*, as previously mentioned, remains one of the most popular books for teens and is highly respected by critics.

Before these books came along, the section of the library devoted to books for teens was filled with junior novels and novels written originally for adults that appealed to young people, like *The Catcher in the Rye* and Hermann Hesse's philosophical and mysterious *Siddhartha* (1962). Besides Zindel and Hinton, only a few other writers emerged during the early years of serious adolescent literature, and these included Judy Blume, Robert Cormier, and Lois Lowry. Ultimately, though, it is Paul Zindel who is most often named as the grandfather of the genre known as young adult (YA) literature. YA novels are typically written from a realistic teenage point of view about realistic teenage experiences. In the world of YA literature, adults are secondary characters at best.

Needless to say, the YA genre that Zindel and his contemporaries created back in the 1960s has expanded in style and subject matter, and continues to flourish. Generally speaking, the average young adult novel focuses on one experience that is common to many modern teenagers, such as peer pressure, divorce, or self-confidence. These books show readers that they are not alone in facing their troubles, and whereas before the 1960s there were no fiction books that discussed teenagers' troubles, there are now hundreds of thousands of YA books and hundreds more are written every year.

To write honestly about troubled adolescents, Zindel returned in his imagination to his own "confused, funny, aching teenage days,"[9] as he later noted. Zindel believed he had more to offer teenagers as a full-time writer than as a science teacher, so he quit teaching in 1969, just months after the publication of his revolutionary first novel, *The Pigman*.

2 Introducing Paul Zindel, Novelist Extraordinaire

Paul Zindel's debut novel takes place on Staten Island, New York, where Zindel was born and raised. (Staten Island is a borough, or division, of New York City, a brief ferry ride away from Manhattan; the other boroughs that comprise New York City are Manhattan, Queens, Brooklyn, and the Bronx.) *The Pigman* is narrated by two fifteen-year-old high school sophomores, John Conlan and Lorraine Jensen. John is moody, cynical, and thrill-seeking, and Lorraine is sensitive, vulnerable, and thoughtful. John is fairly popular but he doesn't really like any of his friends—except Lorraine—and Lorraine has very few other friends. They tell their story in alternating chapters, so the first chapter is from John's point of view, the second is from Lorraine's, then back to John, and so forth. The two have slightly different versions to tell, but their story is essentially the same.

The novel begins with an ominous prologue titled "The Oath."

> Being of sound mind and body on this 15th day of April in our sophomore year at Franklin High School, let it be known that Lorraine Jensen and John Conlan have decided to record the facts, and only the facts about our experience with Mr. Angelo Pignati.
>
> Miss Reillen, the Cricket, is watching us at every moment because she is the librarian at Franklin High and thinks we're using her typewriter to copy a book report for our retarded English teacher.
>
> The truth and nothing but the truth, until this memorial epic is finished, So Help Us God![1]

The "memorial epic" John and Lorraine narrate is not a happy one, though it ends on a bittersweet note. They are writing to explain how they came to befriend and betray a man named Angelo Pignati, a widower whom they met by accident after making a prank phone call to his home. From the first chapter, John and Lorraine admit that Mr. Pignati—whom they call the Pigman because of his large collection of ceramic pigs—has died and that they are at least partially responsible for his death. The mystery of exactly how they caused his death isn't revealed to the reader until the end of the book.

Upon meeting him, John and Lorraine are immediately drawn to Mr. Pignati's childlike enthusiasm and generosity, and he becomes a father figure to the teenagers. John's own parents are cold, critical, and uncommunicative; Lorraine's father left when she was a baby, and her mother is overworked and self-centered. Unlike their parents, Mr. Pignati treats John and Lorraine with respect and talks to them as if they are adults. He offers them wine when they stop by to visit after school and takes them to the zoo to introduce them to Bobo the gorilla, whom he adores. He buys them roller skates and spontaneously encourages them to skate through a department store. He asks about their hopes and dreams and encourages John's ambition of becoming an actor—a plan that John's own father dismisses as silly and unrealistic. Perhaps most important, the Pigman makes the teens feel appreciated, because having them around helps him feel less lonely. The friendship seems to be the perfect cure for Mr. Pignati's depression over his wife's death and for John's and Lorraine's frustrating home lives.

But in the end, John and Lorraine are not up to the task of being Mr. Pignati's faithful friends. After he suffers a mild heart attack and ends up in the hospital, they are left to roam his house alone after school, where they pretend to be grown-ups by cooking dinner, dressing up, and eating by candlelight. This begins innocently enough, but the freedom goes to their heads, and they end up hosting a party that gets out of control. During the party, the Pigman's treasured pig collection is destroyed and the house is trashed. Mr. Pignati returns home to find that his only friends have betrayed him; he is shocked and disappointed and returns to feeling old and lonely.

In an effort to win back Mr. Pignati's affection and trust, John and Lorraine apologize and offer to take him to see Bobo at the zoo. When they arrive, however, Bobo is not in his cage, and a zookeeper coldheartedly announces that the gorilla has died. This is Mr. Pignati's final disappointment, and he immediately suffers a second heart attack and dies. Critics named *The*

Pigman an instant classic, and readers identified immediately with John's and Lorraine's great capacity for joy, pain, love, and frustration. Though Zindel's fans disagree about which of his novels is their favorite, *The Pigman* is generally recognized to be the most popular and widely read.

Twelve years after *The Pigman* hit bookstores and young adult fiction emerged as its own genre, Zindel wrote a sequel called *The Pigman's Legacy* (1980). The sequel picks up two years after Mr. Pignati's death and follows the lives of John and Lorraine as they befriend the elderly, terminally ill man who has moved into the Pigman's former home. The lessons they learned so painfully in the first book are put to good use here, and they realize by the end that the original Pigman's legacy is love, for others and for each other.

Then and Now

Paul Zindel's books might not seem so revolutionary today, but when *The Pigman* was first published, the United States was a somewhat different place. The Vietnam War was going on, and teenagers and

(continued on page 32)

(continued from page 31)

college students made up a large portion of the peace movement, which resulted in a nationwide generation gap. This meant that older people and younger people were having an especially hard time finding common ground and understanding each other. Parents thought their kids were freaks for growing their hair long, for becoming artists instead of professionals, for smoking and cursing openly, and for holding demonstrations to try to gain a voice in the decisions made in their communities and schools. Some parents felt insulted and confused because their kids were questioning the value of traditional institutions, such as school, the government, and family. Young people were also questioning authority figures, including teachers, police, and parents.

The late 1960s also marked a change in popular attitudes toward sex. Young people started to feel free to talk openly about it, to ask questions, and to educate themselves—but still the topic of premarital and teenage sex remains a somewhat thorny issue even decades later. (Zindel's *My Darling, My Hamburger*, which is about teenage sexual activity and the consequences, continues to cause controversy even today.) The year *The Pigman* was published, 1968, was the year that the tensions between young people and their elders reached its breaking point. At the

Democratic National Convention in Chicago that year, where the Democratic Party assembled to announce its nominations for president of the United States, thousands of protesters turned up to demonstrate against the Vietnam War. Violence broke out and many protesters—mostly young people—were injured by police officers.

Enduring Themes

Each of Zindel's young adult novels is unique in many ways, but many share a common sense of realism, honesty, and compassion for adolescent troubles. They also include many of the same themes, or subjects, that Zindel introduced in *The Pigman*. The following are Zindel's major themes.

- *Loneliness and alienation.* Zindel's teenagers are not football quarterbacks or prom queens; they aren't popular or successful or well adjusted. Most of them have few or no friends and have unstable relationships with their parents. Zindel writes about misfits trying to find their place in the world.

- *The generation gap.* Most of Zindel's protagonists have been misled and misunderstood by parents and teachers. As a result, they are skeptical of institutions like school, family, and government, they question authority in general, and they rebel by cursing, drinking, breaking rules, skipping school, and so on.

- *Taking responsibility*. When they are left to fend for themselves in a confusing and challenging world, many of Zindel's characters make bad choices. Only the ones who learn from their mistakes can hold on to a sense of self-worth and make themselves happy.

- *Coping with death and illness*. Many of Zindel's teenagers have lost a parent—usually a father—to physical or mental illness, and others are surrounded by the threat of illness or death. As his characters learn the meaning of life, they also begin to understand the significance of loss.

From Hardship to Horror

The later years of Zindel's career brought about a surprising change in his style and subject matter. Rather than continuing to write about moody, desperate teenagers struggling to survive despite difficult home lives and unhelpful teachers, Zindel took another route entirely. In the early 1990s, he published a string of light-hearted, humorous fiction for the middle grades called Wacky Facts Lunch Bunch series. These books covered the pranks and adventures of five eleven-year-olds.

In the middle and late 1990s, Zindel changed gears again. He returned to writing for a high school audience, but this time he worked on fast-paced adventure novels with fantastical, suspenseful plotlines. Some of these later novels might be accurately called horror books as they contain a good bit of gore and violence.

In an interview, Zindel explained why he changed his writing style so radically.

> I got tired of teenagers having problems. I felt that the problems had all been written about for too long, and that kids were fed up with that posture. It also became somewhat [insincere] for adults to be writing about teenage problems when it's clear how mad and bizarre and foolish and dangerous and stupefying adult life has become.[2]

Though the style changed dramatically, Zindel's books continued to feature clever, resourceful teenagers who knew how to get themselves out of tight spots; the characters were similar in some ways to those of his earlier books, but they lacked the family troubles and other serious obstacles that were a constant in these books. In *Loch*

(1994), Zindel's first adventure book, a gifted fifteen-year-old named Luke Perkins (nicknamed "Loch" because he claimed to have spotted the Loch Ness monster when he was five) teams up with a friend to save a clan of prehistoric sea creatures who live in a local lake. The creatures are being threatened with extinction by a tabloid publisher who wants to use them to sell newspapers. The novel ends with a thrilling face-off between the hunters and the sea creatures.

It gets more exciting from there. *The Doom Stone* (1995) is about a teenager named Jackson Cawley, who, while visiting his aunt in England, hunts down a bloodthirsty ancient half-human beast who comes out of his lair every nineteen years to feed on people. Like *Loch*, *The Doom Stone* received critical praise for its rich use of local scenery, quick pace, and spine-tingling action. *Reef of Death* (1998), which is set in Australia's Great Barrier Reef, is another thrilling horror story where a teenager must defeat a sea beast. *Rats* (1999) is perhaps Zindel's most gory novel. In it, rodents invade New York City after their feeding ground (a garbage dump on Staten Island) is turned into a construction project. The novel includes a vivid scene depicting a man being devoured by a mob of ferocious rats.

Zindel's adventure novels show that he has what it takes to scare readers—really scare them. In an interview, he listed a few things that he finds scary, revealing that a mixture of imagination and realism makes a great writer.

> What frightens me is the thought that I might have a painful, massive heart attack, be shot in a home invasion, or have a rare and barbed tiny Amazon catfish swim into my [bloodstream]. I'm also frightened of my children being injured or shot in a mini-market, being struck by lightning or a meteor, and being devoured feet first by, in order of horror, a crocodile, a great white shark, or a tiger in the swamps of Bengal, and dying of rabies.[3]

In the same way some of these fears are rational and some are irrational, Zindel's adventure novels mix imaginary creatures with real places and people. The layer of realism makes the events in the stories that much more scary. *Raptor* (1998) is a page-turner about a boy's hunt for a baby raptor, which is a carnivorous prehistoric birdlike dinosaur. This excerpt from the book might give you an idea of how Zindel's adventure books combine fantasy with reality to produce frightening situations.

Professor Norak stopped dead in his tracks. This must be a joke, he thought. A few of his paleontology students were playing a joke. Very funny . . .

Two of the summer interns had already shown their twisted senses of humor . . . The professor could easily imagine the same kids stealing into the mine the night before and using chisels to fake the scratching, raking, and kicking marks. He had to laugh. They had made the imprints from talon feet much too large.[4]

The opening two paragraphs from *The Surfing Corpse* (2001) also show Zindel's effective use of suspense, as well as his ability to grab the reader's attention from the start.

It all started about six week ago, with a perfectly normal school trip on a perfectly normal fall day. Of course, when you're talking about our school—Westside School—nothing's ever really normal. Westside is an expensive, private academy, where the students are all either rich, famous, or on some kind of special freaky scholarship. We are probably the [most random] collection of over-privileged, gifted, demented, neurotic teenagers in all of New York City—and when you consider that the city's population is about eight million, that's saying a lot.

The other kids at Westside will tell you that Mackenzie and I are the weird ones. "Wherever they go, people start getting killed left and right," is the buzz going around school these days. And I have to admit, it's sort of true.[5]

In just two paragraphs, Zindel has given readers just enough information to keep them intrigued. Who has died? How is the narrator involved? What exactly started six weeks ago, and what will happen? You have to keep reading to find out.

Among Zindel's later novels, *The Gadget* (2001) combines his taste for fast-paced suspense and action with historical fiction. The story is set in 1945, and in the book, thirteen-year-old Stephen has moved to Los Alamos, New Mexico, where his father, a physicist, is working on a top-secret military "gadget" that seems to make everyone who knows about it very nervous. (Los Alamos is where government scientists developed atomic bombs during World War II.) When Stephen snoops around to learn the gadget's purpose, he sets into motion events that could put him—and the entire country—in extreme danger.

The Gadget is a thriller of the best quality, but it also involves important bits of history—and as exciting and suspenseful as the plot might seem while reading the book, readers will learn that much of it is true. The novel includes a World War II chronology, bibliography, and brief biographies of the central figures who were involved in the development of the atom bomb.

Zindel published seven horror books after *The Gadget*, including *The Surfing Corpse* (2001), *The E-Mail Murders* (2001), *The Square Root of Murder* (2002), and *Death on the Amazon* (2002). He continued to write classic, exciting plots in which brave and intelligent teenagers duel against evil (usually in the form of a gruesome otherworldly creature) and eventually triumph.

Something for Everyone

If the novels Zindel published during his first two decades as a fiction writer are character-driven—meaning that they are focused more on who the story is about than what happens in it—his later adventure books are definitely plot-driven. Considering his books for middle graders, his picture book for young children (*I Love My Mother*, 1975), and his many plays, Zindel has built up quite a diverse résumé. In fact, one might say he has covered all the bases—his work has been adored by serious readers looking for inspiration, reluctant readers looking for a page-turner, little kids looking at picture books, parents who appreciate the theater, and critics of every genre. An entire family might find something written by Zindel for each person to enjoy.

Zindel has been quoted as saying that he wrote for kids who don't like to read, and the American Library Association (ALA) thinks he did it well. Several of his adventure books, including the ones mentioned previously, have been listed on the ALA's Quick Picks for Reluctant Readers. Critics agree that Zindel took care to develop richer characters, settings, and plots than the average horror writer and that his language skills are a cut above. Zindel also was awarded Outstanding Children's Book of the Year citations from the *New York Times* five times over for books written in the first twenty years of his career as a novelist. The ALA awarded him Best Young Adult Book citations for six novels ranging in date from *The Pigman* (1968) to *To Take a Dare* (1982).

3 Truth in Fiction

Paul Zindel has repeatedly acknowledged that many of his novels—especially his more serious books written in the first two decades of his career—incorporate true memories from his own life. In his memoir, or autobiography, *The Pigman & Me* (1992), Zindel answers the question readers have been asking since his first novel debuted twenty years earlier: Who is the real Pigman?

The real Pigman was a cheerful, loving man named Nonno Frankie, the father of Zindel's mother's roommate. Nonno Frankie lived for a short time with Zindel's family in a neighborhood named Travis, on Staten Island. Zindel bonded with Nonno Frankie right away, and the joyful and high-spirited man's presence alleviated the stress of living with his mother, who threatened to commit suicide at least once a month. Nonno Frankie was always joking and laughing. "Remember the three Bs," he would say. "Be careful, be good, and be home early. And never tell a secret to a pig—they're all squealers!"[1]

Nonno made splendid feasts of Sicilian delicacies, taught Zindel how to tie a fish head to the bottom of a crab trap, and how to keep lilies moist in a burlap bag. He gave Zindel advice on how to handle himself in a physical confrontation and taught him to appreciate being unique. He told Zindel to yell "Io sono differente!"—which means "I am different!"—whenever he was feeling glum or having doubts about himself. In an essay about Nonno Frankie, Zindel wrote: "Being different was a plus in his book. It was a thing to be valued. 'Only dead fish swim with the stream,' he'd say. 'Just worry about liking yourself first.'"[2] Zindel never forgot the value of feeling good about himself, and he made sure that the characters he wrote about would learn this lesson as well.

Many other aspects of Zindel's childhood are reflected in his fiction: the lack of long-term friendships, the grueling relationship with his unstable mother, the absence of his father, and low self-esteem. For example, in *The Amazing and Death-Defying Diary of Eugene Dingman* (1987), the main character searches in vain for his absent father. In *My Darling, My Hamburger* (1969), the central characters suffer from low self-esteem, which leads to poor judgment. In *The Pigman*, *The Pigman's Legacy*, and *Harry and Hortense at Hormone High* (1984)—to name a few—characters confront mental and physical illness, a theme that was no doubt inspired by Zindel's eighteen-month convalescence and his mother's psychological problems. In *Confessions of a Teenage Baboon* (1977), the protagonist's mother is a nurse for the terminally ill, as is Lorraine's mother in *The Pigman*, and as was Zindel's mother.

Misfits, Oddballs, and Freaks

All of the major themes that reappear throughout Zindel's novels—loneliness and alienation, the generation gap, taking responsibility, and coping with death and illness—were features of Zindel's childhood. In his books, as in his adolescence, many authority figures are either mentally ill and unstable, materialistic and self-centered, old-fashioned and stubborn, or all of the above.

Rarely do Zindel's books feature a family that communicates openly and expresses love and affection; the home is not a shelter from the cruel, confusing world, but rather a chaotic, unfriendly place that teenagers must escape in order to be accepted and understood.

In *Pardon Me, You're Stepping on My Eyeball!* (1976), fifteen-year-olds Edna Shinglebox and Marsh Mellow are placed in a special education class because of their eccentric behavior. There, they come in contact with other kids who are as distinctive as they are. Eventually, Marsh and Edna learn to value their own eccentricities and each other's.

Zindel holds a special place in his heart for "oddball" teenagers, and it's no secret that he thought of himself as being something of a misfit, especially when he was a lonely, eccentric, introverted adolescent. In a magazine interview, Zindel spoke of his high regard for kids who don't fit in.

I write about misfits, because I was a misfit growing up. I had no father in a time when that was considered freakish. I couldn't catch a baseball. I acted out and got involved in crazy, though relatively harmless, capers. I didn't know who I was or what my career should be. I desperately wanted friends and to be liked, but my family moved around so much I never had the chance to keep many friends. Most of my friends were misfits, too. I think being a misfit is a terrific requisite for becoming an author—becoming creative. When you're not doing so hot in the real world, you invent fictional worlds in which you can have a really spectacular and estimable life.[3]

Teenagers often feel misunderstood by their parents, are suspicious of authority, and are alienated from their peers. This means that teenagers today can still relate to Zindel's timeless characters, even though some were created as many as thirty years ago. In his books, Zindel always identifies with, or takes sides with, the adolescent. It's as if he's rooting for the underdog in any situation, because that's what he was as a teenager.

Because he always wrote from the adolescent point of view, without talking down to or belittling anyone, Zindel's message to his readers comes through loud and clear: Find a way to believe in yourself because you are worth it.

Parents Are Not Always Perfect

Like Zindel in his youth, many of his fictional characters feel an unbridgeable gap between themselves and their parents and teachers. This gap often leads them to rebel in self-destructive ways, such as drinking, smoking, and skipping school. Zindel has been criticized for portraying such behavior in his novels, but he believes that acting out is an inevitable part of adolescence. As he said:

> Teenagers have to rebel. It's part of the growing process. I try to show teens that they aren't alone. I believe I must convince my readers that I am on their side; I know it's a continuous battle to get through the years twelve and twenty—an abrasive time. And so I write always from their own point of view.[4]

Many of Zindel's characters are disappointed when they seek the counsel of adults. In *My Darling, My Hamburger,* Liz asks a teacher for advice on whether to have sex with her boyfriend, who has been pressuring her, but the teacher's advice is unrealistic and worthless, and Liz is left to make the decision alone. Zindel's teenagers are often required to make tough choices without any support from adults, and often they use poor judgment and must then learn from their mistakes.

When they feel misunderstood or neglected by adults, teenagers often begin questioning authority and the value of traditions, such as school, the nuclear family, and the government.

This is the central problem of Zindel's third novel, *I Never Loved Your Mind* (1970). The main characters, seventeen-year-olds Yvette and Dewey, are in some respects typical unhappy and rebellious teenagers, only they've dropped out of school and left home because their parents don't understand them. Yvette is a free spirit who moves from one commune (where lots of unrelated people live together) to another, searching for a place where she can connect with others. Dewey seeks the same kind of connection, particularly with Yvette, but doesn't believe he will find it by moving from one unhappy environment to the next. Although his attempts to form bonds ultimately fail and Yvette turns him away, at the end of the book he finds himself on the brink of learning what life means to him, without the help of his parents' belief system or Yvette's.

Since they are so used to questioning the authority figures in their lives, Zindel's characters often don't recognize the "good" adults from the "bad" ones. John and Lorraine from *The Pigman*, for example, start out treating Mr. Pignati with the same disrespect they show their parents. Lorraine shows some sympathy for one of her teachers, but for the most part, teachers are portrayed as insensitive and unhelpful. The guidance counselor in *Pardon Me, You're Stepping on My Eyeball!* has good intentions but no connection with the kids he wants to help. In *The Pigman*, when John expresses to his parents his desire to be unique, his father yells at him, "Be yourself! Be individualistic! . . . But for God's sake get your hair cut. You look like an oddball!"[5]

Everywhere they turn, Zindel's adolescents come across adults who make little or no effort to see the world through their eyes. If they are fortunate, they find substitute parents, like John and Lorraine find in Mr. Pignati. Otherwise, they are left to figure out life's lessons for themselves.

Turning Lemons into Lemonade

No one knows better than Zindel that the average teenager, in life and in fiction, has a lot on his or her mind. Teens are trying to define their identities, connect with adults and peers, and not mess things up too badly in the process. The problem is that teenagers are human, too, and they are bound to make some errors from time to time. Zindel's characters (parents and kids) are far from perfect—but being perfect isn't the point. The real question is whether they have enough strength and character to take responsibility for themselves, which is often the hardest thing of all. Through his characters, Zindel seems to be saying that if we take responsibility for ourselves, we can hope for a brighter future. If not, we could get stuck and become victims of circumstance.

John and Lorraine in *The Pigman* differ in how much responsibility they will assume in the matter of Mr. Pignati's death. John tends to deflect blame from himself. In the third chapter, he notes:

> Now Lorraine tends to blame all the other things on me, but she was the one who picked out the Pigman's phone number. If you ask me, I think he would have died anyway. Maybe we speeded things up a little, but you can't really say we murdered him. Not murdered him.[6]

But by the end of the book, through the process of writing out his version of what happened, John seems not only to have abandoned his flippant, or dismissive, attitude toward the Pigman's death but also to have learned that his actions do have consequences and that human beings can influence each other's destinies. In the final chapter, he tells of his reaction to Mr. Pignati's death.

> "We murdered him," [Lorraine] screamed, and I turned away because I had been through

just about all I could stand. . . . I wanted to yell at her, tell her he had no business fooling around with kids. I wanted to tell her he had no right going backward. When you grow up, you're not supposed to go back. Trespassing— that's what he had done . . .

We had trespassed, too—been where we didn't belong, and we were punished for it. Mr. Pignati had paid with his life. But when he died something in us had died as well.

There was no one else to blame anymore. No [parents or teachers]. And there was no place to hide . . .

Our life would be what we made of it— nothing more, nothing less.[7]

With the last sentence—"Our life would be what we made of it"—John recognizes that he is responsible for his own life. It would be a shame if he continued to make poor decisions out of rebellion or spite for his parents. As he has been trying to establish, he is an individual, and no one else is to blame for his bad judgment.

Taking responsibility for one's happiness is a lesson Zindel learned firsthand. He grew up lonely and misunderstood, trapped in a home with an abusive and mentally ill mother, but somehow he found a way to survive, and he wanted his characters to do the same. For example, at the end of *The Effect of Gamma Rays on Man-in-the-Moon Marigolds*, Tillie realizes that it is possible to thrive and be happy despite her desperate childhood, as long as she takes on the challenge herself.

Sibella, the main character in *The Girl Who Wanted a Boy*, also finds herself in the position of taking responsibility for her own happiness. After she risks everything and makes a huge sacrifice for Dan, the boy she loves, he rejects her, and she becomes nearly suicidal from the shame of rejection. She has no choice but to act as her own coach or therapist. In healthy families, parents or siblings might console and counsel a teenager in pain, but in situations where there is no familial support, the teenager is left to his or her own resources. This is how it was for Sibella, who has a tough job ahead of her:

> I must recover, she started to tell herself. How can I possibly recover? She began to fight the bad voice inside. She would fight it with small measurements of hope, even though at that moment she didn't believe in hope. Someone will be nice to me. Maybe that's where my mind has to start. Maybe it will be a teacher at school who will say a nice word that isn't too preposterous. Maybe a boy will hold a door for

me. Maybe someone will lend me their umbrella. That's a possibility. I have to fix my heart. I'll get out a different set of tools. I'll stick myself under the binocular microscope. I'll look at my own faults and grow up a little. Just a little. Maybe I can do that. Maybe I can picture myself slightly happy again somewhere.[8]

A Matter of Life and Death

In almost every book, Zindel's teenagers are surrounded by the threat of death or illness. Maybe this comes from Zindel's own experience living in a convalescent home when he was a teenager. Maybe it comes from having a mother who worked with the terminally ill and frequently came home to announce that a patient had died or even to coldly predict that it wouldn't be long before someone did. For whatever reason, Zindel includes death or illness in almost all of his books. In *The Pigman*, before Mr. Pignati actually gets sick and dies, John and Lorraine have already had some experience with death. John has attended the funerals of family members, which he recalls as being boring and uncomfortable. Lorraine has more sensitivity regarding the subject—her mother, like Zindel's own, works with the terminally ill and shows no compassion for her patients. Early in the novel, Lorraine expresses sympathy for a teacher whose dying mother lives in her home. Mr. Pignati tells the teenagers at the start of their friendship that his wife is visiting her sister in California, but they later learn that she is dead and he misses her so badly that he can't accept that she is gone. Despite their familiarity with death, neither John nor Lorraine is prepared for the loss of Mr. Pignati, which is their first experience with true grief.

Confessions of a Teenage Baboon, too, involves illness and death. The protagonist, Chris Boyd, lives with his mother and her ill patient, and although death has always been a peripheral part of his life, he doesn't really understand how it can affect him until the disturbed man who has tried to become a father figure to him takes his own life. The main characters of *Pardon Me, You're Stepping on My Eyeball!* must also face death and start to cope with the permanent loss.

Parents and other adults in many of Zindel's novels have become slightly numbed by death and illness, usually because they have seen so much of it. For Lorraine's mother, death is actually profitable—in addition to working as a nurse, she steals from ill patients and takes bribes from funeral homes for referring her clients to them.

Some of Zindel's adolescents seem to be on the path to becoming the same way, like John, who goes to the cemetery to drink and hang out and thinks of the people buried there as ghouls who might rise from the earth to pull him under. But firsthand experiences with death changes these characters forever and helps them gain a better understanding of human connection.

4 It Pays to Be Distinctive

Tbere are a few features of Zindel's writing style that set him apart from the crowd. One is his fondness for zany titles. Many of his books—especially those written in the first twenty years of his career, before he started writing adventure books— have snappy, slick-sounding, lengthy titles that stick in the mind. Some of them make no sense until after you've read the book, like *My Darling, My Hamburger*, and some reflect the sense of playfulness and humor that is part of Zindel's style, like *The Undertaker's Gone Bananas* (1978). It would have been easier for Zindel to choose titles that wouldn't call so much attention to themselves, but he took the risk and pulled it off—quirky titles became one of his trademarks as a writer. His adventure books, by contrast, have ominous titles that suggest suspense and drama, which suits the genre perfectly. A few examples are *Night of the Bats* (2001), *The Scream Museum* (2001), and *The Square Root of Murder* (2002).

Some of Zindel's characters' names are equally peculiar, like Marsh Mellow, Chris Phlegm, Paranoid Pete, and Joan Hybred, to name a few. Their voices are witty and conversational, though Zindel decided not to include slang in his books. (Slang changes from year to year and could end up making his characters seem old-fashioned). The situations in Zindel's novels aren't as bizarre as the titles or names, but they aren't ordinary either. Generally speaking, Zindel writes about the most intense and challenging moments in adolescence, the times when teenagers find themselves—willingly or not—changing and growing up.

Combining Flash and Class

Unlike his bizarre titles, character names, and situations, Zindel's prose, or writing style, is fairly clear-cut and engaging. In many of his novels, the casual, conversational narration is broken up with notes written in cursive handwriting, lists made by the narrator, and idle doodling. In *The Pigman*, for example, a straightforward chapter narrated by John is suddenly interrupted by a drawing that John has copied from graffiti on his school desk. These fun details provide comic relief from otherwise emotional situations and help to keep the reader's attention. Humor is a major feature in almost all of Zindel's work. His particular comic style is farcical, or absurd. Sometimes his characters' lives seem exaggerated or distorted, which underscores the idea that adolescence is a roller coaster ride during which anything can happen.

Critics often praise Zindel's knack for capturing the authentic voice of the average teenager. His characters perhaps are more clever, sarcastic, and have a more sophisticated vocabulary than many teenagers in real life, but that makes them even more interesting to read about. As previously mentioned, Zindel has written books with dueling narrators (narrators who take turns telling the same story), and he has written from the point of view of females as well as males.

The following is an excerpt from the very beginning of *The Pigman's Legacy*, which is being narrated by John, who is seventeen. Notice the colloquial, or casual, voice and straightforward writing style; it's as if John is telling a story at the dinner table.

> In case you didn't read the first memorial epic Lorraine and I wrote about the Pigman, don't worry about it. I never used to like reading either because a lot of my teachers made me read stuff I didn't need. I may be retarded and selfish but I only like to read things that are going to help me in my life. I mean Lady Macbeth says a lot of brilliant things, but Shakespeare or no Shakespeare, I don't know what she's talking about, and I'm not a stupid boy. Maybe someday I'll be ready for characters like her and Coriolanus and that girl who had to wear the scarlet letter. But right now I find them so boring I could barf. In fact, whenever my English teacher tells me I have to read a book and write a book report about it, I go straight to the library and look for the thinnest book on the shelf.[1]

Again, John shares qualities that the author possessed as a teenager. Zindel explained his experience reading Shakespeare in an interview.

> One author I like now, as an adult, is one I couldn't stand as a high school student— Shakespeare . . . I didn't understand what it was all about. Now, of course, I love him

because I can understand him. And I think the memory of reading things I was not ready for has stayed with me in my own writing. I like to write for kids about worlds they can identify with—worlds they know they're interested in and worlds that have characters who are solving problems that they themselves would want to solve.[2]

From start to finish, readers get the feeling that Zindel's characters reflect a piece of their own lives and that his characters' troubles and triumphs reflect their own. Perhaps this is why Zindel's work continues to be so popular. As critic Jack Forman wrote:

> "Zindel's novels are made-to-order for young adults because they confirm and flesh out two of the most widely held beliefs of adolescents: that they are superior to adults and live more honest lives than they do."[3]

Amid Praise, a Note of Controversy

Critics disagree about which is Zindel's "best" book. Some say *The Pigman*, or *My Darling, My Hamburger*, or *The Pigman's Legacy*, or even *Pardon Me, You're Stepping on My Eyeball!* Readers' favorites vary even more widely, depending on their tastes. If you like mystery, check out *The Undertaker's Gone Bananas*. For horror, gore, and suspense, you may want to read any of Zindel's most recent novels, including *The Doom Stone* and *Rats*. For a more serious—yet still humorous—look at adolescent life, it's worth returning to Zindel's debut novel, *The Pigman*.

Words that are used over and over again to describe Zindel's work include "honest," "empathic" (understanding), "clever," "amusing," and "stimulating." Most critics praise his use of far-fetched plot twists and exaggerated characters, claiming that these things highlight how absurd and confusing "normal" life can be, especially for teenagers. And all critics agree that whether each and every book succeeds, Zindel's work is consistently ambitious, striving to say something important, and—no matter the wacky titles or characters—deserves to be taken seriously.

As you may have noticed, however, many of Zindel's books deal with mature subjects, like drinking, sex, homelessness, and death, which some people find inappropriate topics for kids to read about. Zindel has claimed that teenagers have to face these issues and there's no use trying to hide it from them. Other critics say that Zindel's novels are too dark and depressing, and that the lives of teenagers are not necessarily so grim.

My Darling, My Hamburger is one of Zindel's most controversial books because it deals with the taboo issues of sex and abortion. Liz feels pressured by her boyfriend, Sean, to have sex but is afraid that Sean will lose respect for her if she does what he asks. She is equally afraid of losing him if she doesn't. When she turns to a teacher for advice, the teacher tells Liz that when the topic comes up, she should simply ask Sean out for a hamburger to distract him (hence, the novel's title). This advice strikes Liz as unrealistic and absurd, and she doesn't feel free to speak to her mother and stepfather, so out of desperation she gives in to Sean's advances and, ultimately, becomes pregnant. First, Sean promises to marry her and be the father, then changes his mind. On his father's recommendation, Sean gives Liz money for an abortion. (Abortion was not legal until 1973, which meant that abortions conducted unlawfully prior to that point could be very dangerous.) Maggie, Liz's best friend, accompanies her to the abortion and promises not to tell any adults. However, she is forced to break her promise when Liz suffers from post-surgery complications. In the end, there is a glimmer of hope that all the teenagers involved have learned from the experience.

Many of Zindel's novels have been challenged or banned by groups who believe the books condone, or excuse, violence, premarital sex or abortion, drinking, or other mature activities. A challenge is when a group of parents, community members, or church officials attempts to remove or restrict a book from a school curriculum or library; a ban is the removal of the challenged book. Most challenged books are never removed because concerned parents, teachers, librarians, and other citizens fight to keep the books on library shelves. *The Pigman, Loch,* and *My Darling, My Hamburger* have all wound up on one banned books list or another. In fact, according to the American Library Association, *The Pigman* ranks forty-fourth on the list of the 100 most frequently banned books of all time. (Other authors whose books have been banned include Judy Blume, Richard Peck, Mark Twain, and J. K. Rowling, to name a few.)

There's no question that some of Zindel's books are meant for readers who are sensible and mature enough to understand that the behavior portrayed isn't always responsible, legal, or smart. But Zindel has a lot of faith in adolescents, in fiction, and in life, and he knows that it is up to each individual to take responsibility for his or her actions.

5 An Author's Legacy

wo years before his death in 2003, Zindel arrived at the Winfield School in New Jersey to speak to a group of students about being a writer. When he got there, he noticed that the walls were covered with a variety of handmade pigs, in celebration of his visit. "You have some very original ideas," he told his audience. "You should go with your originality, because that's what's going to make you famous."[1]

Zindel learned this from personal experience. In his everyday life, Zindel was an original but otherwise pretty normal guy. He raised two children with Bonnie Hildebrand, a novelist to whom he was married for twenty-five years, and lived in New York City for most of his adult life. He enjoyed swimming, hiking, fishing, and traveling, and his favorite ice-cream flavor was macadamia nut. He was color-blind and almost always wore a baseball cap. He loved writing books for young adults, he said, because it allowed him to be a kid again and again, and every time he started a new novel he felt like he was being reborn. He also hoped he could help adolescents make sense out of their lives by showing them how his characters get through challenging situations.

For Zindel, inspiration came from anywhere and everywhere. As previously stated, many of his early novels were inspired by real moments from his own adolescence. Later, he would come home from traveling to places such as Indonesia and India and turn the bats and rats he'd seen there into the antagonists of his adventure books. In an interview, he said:

> "Ideas emerge from where I am living, where I am visiting—and most powerfully, from people I meet. I love people. I love kids. The right kid or the right adult will set my mind spinning into an adventure that mesmerizes me for years."[2]

Sadly, Zindel can no longer share his mesmerizing adventures with the world; he died of cancer in New York on March 27, 2003, at the age of sixty-six. Four years earlier, in an interview, Zindel had said:

> "I am such a kid inside I can't imagine realizing that I'm almost old enough to die. I'm certain that death, when it comes, will take me by enormous surprise. I'll probably be getting ready to go on a roller coaster or attend a prom."[3]

Parting Words

Fans of Zindel's work can still read his novels to learn how to write realistically and openly about life. In interviews, Zindel often recommended that writers start all stories out with a bang, or exciting event, to grab the reader's attention. He also recommended more unorthodox methods for learning to write. The following is from an interview he had with Random House.

> Kids like to know how I write. And I do love to give them different hints about writing . . . Sometimes I have them nibble on imaginary chocolate ants and I say, "Now think of all of the adjectives that you're feeling when you're nibbling on those ants." Sometimes I make believe I have a couple of old cow eyeballs in a bag and they have to reach in and feel

those. I try to make kids realize that writing is very [instinctive], it very much depends on our experiences, our senses, and how we can then [transform] those into a story.[4]

Zindel's more serious wisdom about writing reflected his ideas about life, which are embedded in every one of his novels. This wisdom can be simply and clearly stated in four points.

1. Ultimately, good wins over evil.

2. Nature has given human beings the ability to solve problems.

3. There is some meaning and significance to the universe.

4. It is fantastic to be young and involved in the adventure of life.

At the end of his life, Zindel could be confident that not only had he helped revolutionize literature by writing for teenagers in a new, honest, and realistic style, he'd also imparted to his readers the importance of learning from mistakes, appreciating life, understanding the significance of life and death, and making connections with other people. Thirty-five years ago, there were no authors who could claim such an achievement.

It has been said lately that young adult literature is experiencing a steady decline in sales that will continue into the future. This decline is often blamed on the abundance of television talk shows and made-for-television movies and sit-coms, all of which deal with teenage and family troubles and all of which are popular with young adults. This is disappointing news. Any fan of YA literature knows that there's no beating the experience of reading a novel. With a novel, there's no prerecorded laughter interrupting the flow, it isn't finished in an hour or less, and the characters become real people in the reader's imagination. Books like Paul Zindel's, which deal with timeless characters and complicated adolescent dilemmas, last a lifetime in one's memory.

Interview with Paul Zindel

This interview is excerpted from an online interview at Scholastic.com.

SCHOLASTIC: When did you start writing books?

PAUL ZINDEL: I didn't write my first book until 1967, when an editor had seen a play of mine and asked if I had any stories for young people.

SCHOLASTIC: How is writing a novel different from writing a play? Is one easier or harder than the other?

PAUL ZINDEL: For me, a play is easier. It's my most basic talent. It differs strongly from a novel in that nearly all information, all conflict, and most of the plot is carried through dialogue. The other important difference is that in a novel you can actually climb inside a character's head. All that has to be conveyed in dialogue in a play—except for the occasional soliloquy or monologue.

SCHOLASTIC: How does your background in science influence your writing?

PAUL ZINDEL: In science, I learned the scientific method, which makes one approach story-telling with a technique. As writers, we often create our first fiction piece because we've lived it. But after that we have to learn technique. In a sense, my science training really helps me analyze how I did and what I did. It lets me help shape a career. With science, I was accustomed to doing research. Those research techniques have been so useful now that I'm doing some science-fiction novels. Thirdly, we live in a world of science. We live in a world of computers. Our headlines, our TV news are constantly framed in terms of science. I think my training has helped me to keep up with the times and sometimes translate it effectively into fiction.

SCHOLASTIC: What is your favorite part of the writing process?

PAUL ZINDEL: My favorite part is the initial inspiration—when I first glimpse what the fictional animal might be. It's the moment when I read a headline that boggles my mind. Or, when a kid tells me about something startling that happened to him or her. Or when I find myself in the middle of a breathtaking adventure or romance.

SCHOLASTIC: What inspired you to write *The Pigman?*

PAUL ZINDEL: I was living in a fifty-room empty castle on Staten Island. I was minding it for a real estate firm. I was thirty years old at the time. One day, a teenage boy trespassed across the grounds. I went out to scold him, but he turned out to be one of the most interesting young men I'd ever met. He told me a lot of the exciting adventures that appeared in *The Pigman.* I modeled Lorraine after a girl (named Lorraine) who was a student in one of the chemistry classes that I was teaching at Tottenville High School. She was a girl who used to cry anytime anything about death, dying, or war was mentioned. I thought, what a wonderful adventure it would be to team those two life models into a story in which they met an eccentric, old mentor figure.

Mr. Pignati was based on an Italian grandfather that I knew.

SCHOLASTIC: Why did you choose to have Lorraine and John both narrate *The Pigman* rather than just one of them?

PAUL ZINDEL: I think there are two reasons. First, I think boys like to read about a male protagonist and I think girls like to read stories in which a young girl is the main character. I wanted as large an audience as possible for my book. So, I chose to use these dual protagonists to tell my story. And it's worked out that both boys and girls enjoy the book. My second reason for using dual protagonists was because, I believe, without knowing it, I was psychologically equipped to record both the male and female point of view for *The Pigman.*

SCHOLASTIC: Are you more like Lorraine, John, or the Pigman, and why?

PAUL ZINDEL: In order to make any character believable, you have to put a piece of yourself into each of them. So, there's a part of me that's Lorraine, there's a part of me that's John, and there's a part of me that's the Pigman. I think this also gets at what makes for the existence of a writer. Writers are like chameleons. They don't really survive unless they are able to adjust, change, and transform into many, many worlds.

SCHOLASTIC: How did you come up with the name Pignati? Does it have any special significance?

PAUL ZINDEL: First, I decided that I wanted the lead character to collect pigs. Second, I wanted the lead character to be Italian. I realized years later that the reason was that an Italian grandfather named Nonno Frankie became a surrogate father for me, my sister, and his own grandchildren. This is a tale I've told in great detail in *The Pigman & Me*.

SCHOLASTIC: Were you a writer in grade school?

PAUL ZINDEL: I did create fictional worlds by using puppets and putting on ghost shows— scary shows, which would be inhabited by goblins, ghosts, and elements of life that would be surprising and startling. It wasn't until high school that I began to write actual essays and short stories and plays.

SCHOLASTIC: What advice do you have for . . . students who want to be writers?

PAUL ZINDEL: First, of course, it's wonderful to write about what you know. About your family, about yourself and your friends. Write about those things that make you laugh or cry deeply. Start your story with a bang—a good title, a fascinating opening sentence and paragraph. Create a lead character that audiences can identify with and will want to go on a journey with. Make certain that there's a villain of equal and frightening strength to create conflict for the protagonist. Make certain that the hero wants something, that he has a goal, or you will end up with a shopping list and not a story. Make certain that there are surprises and reversals, that there are unexpected things that happen. One writer said, when your story is getting boring, make sure you drop a corpse through the roof. Have your hero or heroine learn something. Perhaps it will be an epiphany [a sudden understanding of the meaning of something]—an insight into themselves, or an insight into someone else, or into the world. And remember, most people want to read about, and most publishers want to publish, and most movie companies want to buy, stories in which the hero wins against the terrible villain.

SCHOLASTIC: Did you keep a journal for your thoughts when you were growing up? Do you keep one now?

PAUL ZINDEL: Yes. I keep a journal, like many writers do. But the journal has changed its shape. I realize now that a journal is not just a collection of random written notes. Now, thanks to modern technology, it can also contain snippets of tape recordings, photos, video excerpts, stills from movies, poems, a myriad of images and jottings, magazine clippings, and newspaper articles. I set down those things that make me laugh or cry. These all become fodder for additional stories.

SCHOLASTIC: Through your years of writing, what skills have you learned? Has your writing process changed over the years?

PAUL ZINDEL: Yes. What I've learned is, one, you cannot write a great novel or play or any work of fiction without extraordinary technique—something you learn in school from teachers and librarians—and two, at some point in the creative process you must forget the technique and fly. I've learned that great writing, which I hope to achieve one day, has to be a combination of those two things—of extraordinary technique and courageous chaos.

SCHOLASTIC: When you are writing, do you have to sort of think like a kid to be able to really get into the heads of the children in the book?

PAUL ZINDEL: Yes. The best young adult and children's writers have portions of themselves that are still very much back at the age they're writing from. I've never met a young adult or children's writer who has fully grown up. They retain the ability to at least be childlike.

SCHOLASTIC: Do you think you will always write?

PAUL ZINDEL: Yes! Everyone else gets to retire. Writers never retire, because their minds are constantly needing to create fictional worlds in which they can become alive. Writing is a dream; it doesn't stop until death. And even then, maybe it still goes on!

SCHOLASTIC: Is it sometimes hard to think of a story?

PAUL ZINDEL: Yes. I don't believe in writer's block. I believe in "writer's abyss." That means that you have to fill yourself back up again. The way a writer does that is to call friends, go see movies and plays, take trips to Tahiti and Borneo, eat plenty of ice cream and pizza, and have a wonderful time. So, the next time if any kid is late with their assignment, they should tell their teacher that they need a bigger budget in order to refill. Sometimes a trip to a museum or reading a wonderful book is in order.

SCHOLASTIC: What other books do you like to read besides your own books?

PAUL ZINDEL: I have to read a lot of books in preparation for writing a novel. This past year I've read a lot of books about rats. I'm working on another book about the atomic bomb. So, I've had to read a lot of books about Los Alamos, on radioactivity, on fictional and true accounts about the development of the atomic bomb. I've had to read extensively about World War II. I've had to read about President Franklin D. Roosevelt and President Harry Truman and Adolf Hitler. When you decide to write a book, along with it comes a lot of research that you must do. For pleasure, I read books about topics that really interest me. I read books about male and female relationships. I like reading other young adult writers—Patricia MacLachlan, Paula Danziger, Liz Levy, for example. Along with them I read people like Tom Wolfe and any topic that grabs my interest and attention. I also like reading books on fishing.

Timeline

May 15, 1936 Paul Zindel is born on Staten Island to parents Paul and Beatrice.

1951 Zindel contracts tuberculosis at the age of fifteen and is placed in a convalescent home for eighteen months.

1954 Zindel graduates from high school and enrolls as a chemistry major at Wagner College on Staten Island.

1959 The second play Zindel wrote, *Dimensions of Peacocks*, is performed on stage in New York.

1960 Zindel begins teaching physics and chemistry at Tottenville High School on Staten Island.

1964 Zindel's fourth play, *The Effect of Gamma Rays on Man-in-the-Moon*

Marigolds, opens at the Alley Theater in Houston.

1966 *Marigolds* is made into a television movie; book editor Charlotte Zolotow contacts Zindel to encourage him to write a book for teenagers.

1968 Zindel publishes his revolutionary first novel, *The Pigman*.

1969 Zindel leaves teaching to write full-time.

1971 *Marigolds* opens to rave reviews on Broadway in New York City, then wins the Pulitzer Prize in drama.

1992 Zindel publishes his only memoir, *The Pigman & Me*.

1994 After twenty-five years of success, Zindel publishes *Loch*, a fast-paced adventure story for teenagers that signals a departure from Zindel's earlier work.

2002 Zindel is awarded the Young Adult Library Service Association's Margaret A. Edwards Award, which honors lifelong and enduring excellence in writing for young adults, as well as the Assembly on Literature for Adolescents Award for his contributions to YA literature.

2003 Zindel dies of cancer at Beth Israel Medical Center in Manhattan on March 27.

Selected Reviews from *School Library Journal*

The Doom Stone
1995

Gr 7–10—While driving past Stonehenge on his way to visit his anthropologist aunt, Jackson, fifteen, sees a creature mauling a young man. It turns out that Aunt Sarah is leading a team of scientists and military personnel who are investigating a series of mutilations in the area. Jackson tags along as the monster is sighted and manages several narrow escapes. The creature, actually an intelligent and blood-thirsty hominid living beneath Salisbury Plain, kills several people, and Zindel describes the deaths in gruesome detail. The action and thrills are nonstop, but the hunt for the beast poses moral dilemmas, too. Jackson and his friend Alma discover a similar but harmless new species as well, and Jackson wants to keep them a secret. At times the plot is contrived. It seems unlikely that Jackson would really be asked to take part in the search, or that he and Alma could travel so freely about in a conveniently available dune buggy without being spotted. But the intriguing premise and suspenseful, fast-paced action will surely please readers who like horror stories with a bit more substance than the latest Pike or Stine.

The Gadget
March 2001

Gr 6–9—A suspenseful and fast-paced read. In 1944, thirteen-year-old Stephen is living in London amid the constant threat of German air raids that have already taken the life of his favorite cousin and soul mate. Fearing for his safety, Stephen's mother sends him by boat, then train, to join his father, an American physicist, in Los Alamos, New Mexico. The boy's new home is on "Bathtub Row" of "Site Y," a tightly secured military base surrounded by high fences and attentive guards. Anxious to be united with his father, he is disappointed to find the man distracted and tired from working on a project he is unwilling to discuss. The mystery enveloping the base piques Stephen's curiosity and he accidentally ends up in the hospital room of a dying man who warns him about "the gadget." He is befriended by an older boy and, in a dramatic climax, they secretly follow the scientists off base and witness a horrific explosion, the first atomic bomb test on July 16, 1945, in the Jornada del Muerto Desert. In an epiphany, Stephen realizes the magnitude of this event and through his eyes, so do readers. Zindel's attention to historical accuracy is evident throughout. Unfortunately, Stephen's story is not as carefully crafted. Special circumstances and conveniences allow him to always be in the right place at the right time and a few incidents strain credibility. Overall, though, this book is an exciting introduction to the time period.

Loch
1995

Zindel draws on his scientific background in this story of Luke Perkins, fifteen, nicknamed "Loch" after claiming to see a lake monster as a little boy. He and his younger sister, Zaidee, join their oceanographer father on an expedition searching for enormous prehistoric creatures sighted in Lake Alban in Vermont. Their leader, Cavenger, is a ruthless despot who would just as soon annihilate as preserve the Plesiosaurs, water beasts thought to be extinct for over 10 million years. The siblings and Cavenger's daughter befriend Wee Beastie and help it and its family escape to safety; Dr. Perkins, who has been diminished in his own and his childrens' eyes by selling out his ideals in his need for money, redeems himself. The book is really about what makes a family, whether human or creature, as Loch and Zaidee adjust to their mother's death and help their father regain his self-respect. The gruesome attacks by Plesiosaurs on some humans are gory and grisly enough to satisfy even the blood-thirstiest of middle schoolers. Zindel's style capably blends descriptive, figurative language with YA dialogue.

The Pigman & Me
September 1992

Gr 7–12—Thousands of YAs have read and loved Zindel's *The Pigman* (HarperCollins, 1968). In this tragicomic memoir, he describes one of his own teen years spent with his mother and sister on Staten Island. He is in rare form here. While he's not the first to turn teenage angst into humor, he is certainly among the best. His neurotic, wheeler-dealer mother talks her way into purchasing a house with Connie, another single mother, who has a set of out-of-control, identical twins. Travis is a very insular town, consisting largely of Polish families, and Zindel's one friend, Jennifer Wolupopski, warns him of the less-than-cordial reception he's bound to receive in September. His fears are somewhat soothed when he meets Connie's father, who is destined to become his pigman. He is the first male adult who listens to the boy, laughs with him, and really loves him. Always telling silly jokes and working in Connie's garden, he is never too busy to talk to and advise Zindel on the important things in life, such as how to get fried killies and how to win his first fistfight. The old man changes his life, making it more bearable when his spirit could have been crushed by his family situation. *The Pigman & Me* allows readers a glimpse of Zindel's youth, gives them insight into some of his fictional characters, and provides many examples of universal experiences that will make them laugh and cry.

Raptor
1998

A page-turner for older dinosaur lovers. While exploring a cave alone, Zack's paleontologist father is seriously wounded when he encounters a female raptor guarding her nest. After he is rescued, Zack goes to the area and finds a dinosaur egg, whereupon he is faced with circumstances that force him to make some very difficult choices. Add to this, an ego-maniacal professor, a Native-American friend and her wise grandmother, and highly descriptive prose, and the result is a teen perspective of *Jurassic Park*. If readers can survive the violent opening scene, they will enjoy equally descriptive encounters throughout the rest of the book. Although gory, these vivid portrayals make the narrative effective. Zindel is a master at creating and sustaining a mood and *Raptor* is no exception. From beginning to end, young people will be immersed in a battle between animal and man. In addition, the author adds to the plot by juxtaposing this encounter with society's fascination with sensationalism and materialistic nature. If Zack can capture a living dinosaur, his father will be a celebrity. There are several layers to this story and readers can determine for themselves how deep they will delve. The imaginative ending offers an opportunity for discussion about mutation and animal freedom.

Rats
1999

Staten Island and the rest of New York City are threatened by an invasion of vicious killer rats in this gory, makes-your-skin-crawl thriller. The epicenter of the disaster turns out to be a huge landfill brimming over with decades worth of rotting garbage, right next to the quiet neighborhood where Sarah Macafee, fifteen, and her brother, Michael, ten, live with their widowed father. Mr. Macafee just happens to be the city sanitation officer in charge of the landfill, which is in the process of being paved over with a layer of asphalt. The horror begins one summer morning with rats emerging from residents' toilets, hot tubs, and in-ground swimming pools. Sarah and Michael discover a neighbor dead in her car, and alert their father that rodents from the landfill are mounting an attack on their neighborhood. Readers looking for gruesome details are treated to numerous descriptions of bodily dismemberment by these traditionally maligned mammals, and the jolts of horror recur at regular intervals while Sarah and her brother survive several cliffhanger escapes. Just in the nick of time, Sarah figures out a way to halt the vermin in their tracks and put an end to the bloodbath that engulfs a crowded Manhattan entertainment center. Zindel's style is fast-paced and the plot is chock-full of shivery, stomach-churning action. Young readers will certainly rest easier once Sarah uses her wits to end a nightmare of carnage.

List of
Selected Works

The Amazing and Death-Defying Diary of Eugene Dingman. New York: Harper & Row, 1987.

A Begonia for Miss Applebaum. New York: Harper & Row, 1989.

Confessions of a Teenage Baboon. New York: Harper & Row, 1977.

The Doom Stone. New York: HarperCollins Children's Books, 1995.

The Effect of Gamma Rays on Man-in-the-Moon Marigolds. New York: Harper & Row, 1971.

The E-Mail Murders. New York: Hyperion Books for Children, 2001.

The Gadget. New York: HarperCollins Children's Books, 2001.

The Girl Who Wanted a Boy. New York: Harper & Row, 1981.

Harry and Hortense at Hormone High. New York: Harper & Row, 1985.

I Never Loved Your Mind. New York: Harper & Row, 1970.

The Lethal Gorilla. New York: Hyperion Books for Children, 2001.

Loch. New York: HarperCollins Children's Books, 1994.

My Darling, My Hamburger. New York: Harper & Row, 1969.

Night of the Bat. New York: Hyperion Books for Children, 2001.

Pardon Me, You're Stepping on My Eyeball! New York: Harper & Row, 1976.

The Pigman. New York: Harper & Row, 1968.

The Pigman & Me. New York: HarperCollins, 1992.

The Pigman's Legacy. New York: Harper & Row, 1980.

Raptor. New York: Hyperion Books for Children, 1998.

Rats. New York: Hyperion, 1999.

Reef of Death. New York: HarperCollins Children's Books, 1998.

The Scream Museum. New York: Hyperion Books for Children, 2001.

The Surfing Corpse. New York: Hyperion Books for Children, 2001.

The Undertaker's Gone Bananas. New York: Harper & Row, 1978.

List of
Selected Awards

Assembly on Literature for Adolescents
  Award (2002)
Ford Foundation Grant for Drama (1967)
Margaret A. Edwards Award honoring his
  lifetime contribution in writing for
  young adults (2002)

Confessions of a Teenage Baboon (1977)
Best Young Adult Books citation, American
  Library Association (1977)

**The Effect of Gamma Rays on Man-in-the-
  Moon Marigolds (1963)**
New York Drama Critics Award for Best
  American Play of the Year (1970)
New York Critics Award (1971)

Pulitzer Prize in Drama (1971)
Best Young Adult Books citation, American
    Library Association (1971)

I Never Loved Your Mind (1970)
Outstanding Children's Book of the Year
    citation, *New York Times* (1970)

My Darling, My Hamburger (1969)
Outstanding Children's Book of the Year
    citation, *New York Times* (1969)

Pardon Me, You're Stepping on My Eyeball! (1976)
Best Young Adult Books citation, American
    Library Association (1976)
Outstanding Children's Book of the Year
    citation, *New York Times* (1976)

The Pigman (1968)
Children's Book of the Year, Child Study
    Association of America (1968)
Award for Text, *BostonGlobe/Horn Book* (1969)
Best Young Adult Books citation, American
    Library Association (1975)

The Pigman's Legacy (1980)
Best Young Adult Books citation, American
    Library Association (1980)

Outstanding Children's Book of the Year
citation, *New York Times* (1980)

To Take a Dare (1982)

Best Young Adult Books citation, American
Library Association (1982)

The Undertaker's Gone Bananas (1978)

Outstanding Children's Book of the Year
citation, *New York Times* (1978)

Glossary

abrasive Irritating or rough.

anguish Extreme pain or anxiety; despair.

borough A division or section.

caper An illegal or questionable act; an escapade.

character-driven When the character is more important to a story than the plot.

condone To pardon or excuse.

convalescent home A place where ill people stay while recovering.

cyclorama A round or semicircular diorama or stage setting.

debut The first appearance.

eccentric Being unconventional in an odd or quirky way; also, a person who is unconventional in an odd or quirky way.

empathic Being understanding or sympathetic.

evangelist A person who preaches his or her beliefs to others.

fantastical Imaginary or unrealistic.

farcical Satirical or intentionally silly.

fatigue Extreme exhaustion.

flippant Offhand or careless.

frivolous Lacking in significance or meaning.

generation gap The differing perspectives of teenagers from their parents and teachers, or the differences between any generations.

genre A type or kind of art, literature, or music.

insufferable Unbearable.

introvert Someone who prefers to be alone or lacks social skills.

Loch Ness monster A legendary sea creature that supposedly inhabits a lake in Scotland.

memoir An autobiography.

metaphor When one thing is used to symbolize or represent something else.

naive Innocent and inexperienced.

narrate To tell a story.

nostalgic Longing for the past.

ominous Foreboding, menacing, or threatening.

peace movement In the 1960s and 1970s, the effort of U.S. citizens to end the war in Vietnam.

pining Wishing or desiring.

pioneer A person who starts a new trend.

plot The storyline.

plot-driven When the plot is more important to a story than the characters.

point of view Perspective.

posture Position, opinion, or stance.

preposterous Outrageous or unbelievable.

prose The language of novels and nonfiction books.

protagonist The main character with whom the reader identifies.

revolutionary Being groundbreaking or highly innovative.

science fiction Set in the future or in a fantasy world.

self-destructive Being harmful to oneself.

skeptical Doubtful.

stereotype A standard, overused, and usually inaccurate mental image of a group of people.

taboo Forbidden or unmentionable.

terrarium An enclosure for keeping small animals or plants.

theme The ideas in a novel or story that reappear in different forms.

tuberculosis (TB) A contagious disease that resides in the lungs.

unorthodox Nontraditional.

Vietnam War A war against Communism that the United States took part in from roughly 1965 through 1975.

young adult (YA) A genre of literature aimed at adolescents and teenagers.

For More Information

Web Sites

Due to the changing nature of Internet links, the Rosen Publishing Group, Inc., has developed an online list of Web sites related to the subject of this book. This site is updated regularly. Please use this link to access the list:

http://www.rosenlinks.com/lab/pzin

For Further Reading

Berger, Laura Standley. *Twentieth-Century Young Adult Writers*. Farmington Hills, MI: St. James Press, 1994.

Children's Literature Review. Vol. 3. Detroit: Gale Group, 1978.

Hedblad, Alan, ed. *Something About the Author*. Vol. 102. Detroit: Gale Group, 2000.

Bibliography

Aronson, Marc. "When Coming of Age Meets the Age That's Coming." *Voice of Youth Advocates*, Vol. 21, No. 4. October 1998, pp. 261–263.

Berger, Laura Standley. *Twentieth-Century Young Adult Writers*. Farmington Hills, MI: St. James Press, 1994.

Berkin, George. "Obituaries: Author Paul Zindel." *Newark Star-Ledger*, March 28, 2003.

Children's Literature Review. Vol. 3. Detroit: Gale Group, 1978.

Hedblad, Alan, ed. *Something About the Author*. Vol. 102. Detroit: Gale Group, 2000.

Lesesne, Terri. "Humor, Bathos, and Fear: An Interview with Paul Zindel." *Teacher Librarian*, Vol. 27, No. 2, December 1999, pp. 60–62.

Mitchell, Sean. "Grown-up Author's Insights into Adolescent Struggles." *Dallas Times Herald*, June 27, 1979.

Roback, Diane, and Joy Bean. "Adding Up the Numbers." *Publishers Weekly*, February 10, 2003.

Scholastic Books. "Authors and Books: Biography of Paul Zindel." Scholastic, 2001. Retrieved March 2003 (http://www2. scholastic.com/teachers/authorsandbooks/ authorstudies/authorstudies.html).

Zindel, Paul. "About This Author." Random House, 2002. Retrieved March 2003 (http://www.randomhouse.com/teachers/ authors/zind.html).

Zindel, Paul. *The Effect of Gamma Rays on Man-in-the-Moon Marigolds*. New York: Harper & Row, 1971.

Zindel, Paul. *The Girl Who Wanted a Boy*. New York: Harper & Row, 1981.

Zindel, Paul. "Journey to Meet the Pigman." *The Alan Review*, Vol. 22, No. 1, Fall 1994.

Zindel, Paul. *The Pigman*. New York: Harper & Row, 1968.

Zindel, Paul. *The Pigman's Legacy*. New York: Harper & Row, 1980.

Zindel, Paul. *Raptor*. New York: Hyperion Books for Children, 1998.

Zindel, Paul. *The Surfing Corpse*. New York: Hyperion Books for Children, 2001.

"Zindel Having Problems and Lots of Fun, Too." *Morning Telegraph*, July 30, 1970. Reprinted in *Something About the Author*, Alan Hedblad, ed., Vol. 102. Detroit: Gale Group, 2000.

Source Notes

Chapter 1

1. Paul Zindel, "About This Author." Random House, 2002. Retrieved March 2003 (http://www.randomhouse.com/teachers/authors/zind.html).
2. "Zindel Having Problems and Lots of Fun, Too," *Morning Telegraph*, July 30, 1970. Reprinted in *Something About the Author*, Alan Hedblad, ed., Vol. 102 (Detroit: Gale Group, 2000), p. 227.
3 Paul Zindel, "About This Author."
4. Ibid.
5. Scholastic Books, "Authors and Books: Biography of Paul Zindel." Scholastic, 2001. Retrieved March 2003 (http://www2.scholastic.com).
6. Ibid.

7. Sean Mitchell, "Grown-up Author's Insights into Adolescent Struggles," *Dallas Times Herald*, June 27, 1979.

8. Terri Lesesne, "Humor, Bathos, and Fear: An Interview with Paul Zindel," *Teacher Librarian*, Vol. 27, No. 2, December 1999, pp. 60–62.

9. Sydney Fields, "Author Has Chemistry for Kids," *Daily News* (New York), March 9, 1978.

Chapter 2

1. Paul Zindel, *The Pigman* (New York: Harper & Row, 1968), prologue.

2. Terri Lesesne, "Humor, Bathos, and Fear: An Interview with Paul Zindel," *Teacher Librarian*, Vol. 27, No. 2, December 1999, pp. 60–62.

3. Ibid.

4. Paul Zindel, *Raptor* (New York: Hyperion, 1998), p. 1.

5. Paul Zindel, *The Surfing Corpse* (New York: Hyperion, 2001), p. 1.

Chapter 3

1. Paul Zindel, "Journey to Meet the Pigman," *The Alan Review*, Vol. 22, No. 1, Fall 1994.

2. Ibid.

3. Terri Lesesne, "Humor, Bathos, and Fear: An Interview with Paul Zindel," *Teacher Librarian*, Vol. 27, No. 2, December 1999, pp. 60–62.

4. Scholastic Books, "Authors and Books: Biography of Paul Zindel." Scholastic, 2001. Retrieved March 2003 (http://www2. scholastic.com).

5. Paul Zindel, *The Pigman* (New York: Harper & Row, 1968), p. 60.

6. Ibid., p. 18.

7. Ibid., pp. 147–148.

8. Paul Zindel, *The Girl Who Wanted a Boy* (New York: Harper & Row, 1981), p. 145.

Chapter 4

1. Paul Zindel, *The Pigman's Legacy* (New York: Harper & Row, 1980), p. 1.

2. Paul Zindel, "About This Author." Random House, 2002. Retrieved March 2003 (http://www.randomhouse.com/teachers /authors/zind.html).

3. Laura Standley Berger, *Twentieth-Century Young Adult Writers* (Farmington Hills, MI: St. James Press, 1994).

Chapter 5

1. George Berkin, "Obituaries: Author Paul Zindel," *Newark Star-Ledger*, March 28, 2003.

2. Terri Lesesne, "Humor, Bathos, and Fear: An Interview with Paul Zindel," *Teacher Librarian*, Vol. 27, No. 2, December 1999, pp. 60–62.

3. Ibid.

4. Paul Zindel, "About This Author." Random House, 2002. Retrieved March 2003 (http://www.randomhouse.com/teachers/authors/zind.html).

Index

About the Author

Susanna Daniel is a freelance copywriter and editor, and an adjunct instructor of creative writing at the University of Wisconsin-Madison. Her fiction has been published in *Best New American Voices 2001*, published by Harcourt, as well as *Epoch Magazine* and the *Madison Review*. She is at work on a novel set in her hometown of Miami, Florida.

Photo Credits

Cover © Roger Ressmeyer/Corbis; p. 2 © AP/World World Photos.

Designer: Tahara Hasan; Editor: Annie Sommers